My Pony Book

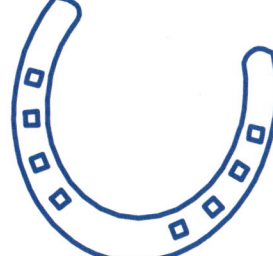

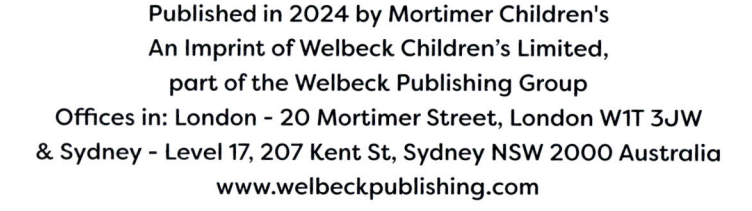

Published in 2024 by Mortimer Children's
An Imprint of Welbeck Children's Limited,
part of the Welbeck Publishing Group
Offices in: London - 20 Mortimer Street, London W1T 3JW
& Sydney - Level 17, 207 Kent St, Sydney NSW 2000 Australia
www.welbeckpublishing.com

Design and layout © Welbeck Children's Limited 2024
Text copyright © Welbeck Children's Limited 2024

All rights reserved. No part of this publication may be reproduced, stored in a retrieval system, or transmitted in any form or by any means, electronically, mechanical, photocopying, recording or otherwise, without the prior permission of the copyright owners and the publishers.

ISBN 978 1 83935 254 6

Printed in Dongguan, China

10 9 8 7 6 5 4 3 2 1

Disclaimer: Any names, characters, trademarks, service marks and trade names detailed in this book is the property of their respective owners and are used solely for identification and reference purposes. This book is a publication of Welbeck Children's Limited, part of Welbeck Publishing Group and has not been licensed, approved, sponsored or endorsed by any person or entity.

Author: Caroline Rowlands
Designer: Kathryn Davies
Design Manager: Sam James
Editor: Joff Brown
Production: Melanie Robertson

My Pony Book

All about horses and ponies!

MORTIMER

SADDLE UP!

Get ready for a pony-tastic adventure inside this fun book.

It's bursting with top tips on how to care for, train, and ride your pony, plus get the lowdown on all the different pony breeds and colors. By the time you get to the last page, you'll *neigh* everything there is to know about horses and be a pony expert!

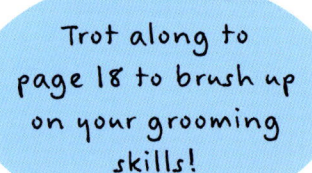

Trot along to page 18 to brush up on your grooming skills!

Pony Know-How	6
Horse Breeds	8
Cool Colors	10
Perfect Points	12
Making Friends	14
Horsin' Around	16
Great Grooming	18
Home Sweet Home	20
Pony People	22
Top Tack	24
Training Tips	26
Ready to Ride	28
Mounting Your Pony	29
Groundwork	30
Scrub Up	31
Giddy Up!	32
The Great Outdoors	34
Showtime	36

There are 20 more of these lucky horseshoes hidden in the book. Can you spot them all?

Super Speed	38
10 Tidy Tips	40
Super Stars	42
Healthy Horses	44
How to Draw a Pony	45
My Perfect Pony	46

Follow me to page 33 to learn how to canter!

PONY KNOW-HOW

Horses and ponies are amazing animals and each one is unique, just like us.

Ever wondered what the difference is between a horse and a pony? It's all about its size and body shape.

Taller than 14.2 hands = horse
14.2 hands or shorter = pony
14.2 hands is about 58 inches.

Ponies also tend to have plumper bodies and stockier legs.

Horses and ponies are measured from the ground to the top of their withers, which is the highest point of their backs.

Ponies and horses have helped humans in lots of different ways throughout history, from working down mines and on farms, to delivering the mail, helping the police force, and working as therapy animals. Smart and loyal, they are very useful and much loved all around the world.

A baby horse is called a foal until it is 1 year old, after that it is called a yearling.

A female foal is called a filly and a male foal is called a colt.

When they turn 4, male horses are called geldings or stallions and female horses are called mares.

ha ha!
What did the mother horse say to her foal?

It's way *pasture* bedtime!

Ponies and horses can live up to 30, or sometimes even 40 years.

DID YOU KNOW?
A foal can stand up and run around just hours after it's born.

HORSE BREEDS

There are hundreds of different breeds of horses and ponies and they come in all shapes and sizes.

The Pony of the Americas is perfect for young riders, as it is a gentle and intelligent breed.

Don't be fooled by the small size of the Shetland Pony. It may be cute, but it is also super strong.

A distinct head shape and a high tail make it easy to recognize the impressive Arabian breed of horse.

Thoroughbred horses are known for their agility and speed while the Appaloosa is famous for its spotted pattern and gentle, loyal nature.

The American Quarter Horse is one of the most popular breeds thanks to its quick speed over short distances.

One of the tallest and strongest horse breeds is the Shire horse. In the past, these huge horses were used to pull wagons and equipment for transport and farming.

The tiny Falabella horse is only around 6 hands tall, but is known as a miniature horse rather than a pony!

Falabella horse   Shire horse

COOL COLORS

There are four basic colors that make up a horse's coat: black, bay (reddish-brown), chestnut, and gray. The mixing of these creates a huge variety of impressive coat colors.

Buckskin

Palomino

Red roan

Flaxen chestnut

Dun

Blue-eyed cream

Which one do you like best?

Horses and ponies have lots of unusual patterns too.

Dapple gray

Piebald

Appaloosa

Tobiano

Overo

Leopard

DID YOU KNOW?

Horses can't burp as they breathe through their noses, not their mouths.

Can you cross out every letter that appears twice to reveal the name of a horse breed that looks like it has been splashed with paint?

P C I R N L Q C T Q R L O

Answer: PINTO

PERFECT POINTS

The parts of a horse's and pony's body are called points. There are a lot to learn, but knowing them is an important part of taking care of any pony.

- dock
- tail
- hock
- cannon
- pastern
- gaskin

The rounded middle part of a horse is called the barrel.

withers crest poll

forehead

muzzle

throat larch

knee

fetlock

coronet

hoof

ha ha!
What did the horse say when it fell over?

I can't *giddy up!*

DID YOU KNOW?
Horses have around 205 bones in their bodies.

13

MAKING FRIENDS

Check out these top tips to help you and your pony bond and remain best friends forever.

If your pony doesn't like being cuddled, give them a gentle rub instead.

Be patient with your pony and remain calm at all times.

Always be kind to your pony.

Take time to talk to your pony so it gets used to your voice.

True or false?
A horse's teeth take up more space in its head than its brain does.

Get to know your pony and its likes and dislikes. When you find out what your pony likes, use it to reward them.

Pay attention to your pony and listen to what it's trying to tell you.

Answer: TRUE

Don't make your pony do things—figure out how to help them to do things.

In the wild, horses and ponies use their teeth to scratch each other's itches. By brushing your pony, you will be scratching their itches and soothing them.

Respect your pony's space and approach it quietly and carefully.

Try to do things in the same way. This will help build trust and reassure your pony.

Always make sure your pony has plenty of food and water.

ha ha!
When does a horse talk?

Whinny wants to!

DID YOU KNOW?
Horses have the largest eyes of all land mammals.

HORSIN' AROUND

You can tell a lot about your pony or horse, just by watching their behavior and body language.

Ponies and horses are herd animals and tend to stick together for protection and company.

A dangling lower lip is a sign that your pony is relaxed and happy.

If you spot your pony swooshing its tail, it could be trying to swat a fly, or warn off another pony who is getting too close.

If your pony flares its nostrils, it could be trying to inhale more air or it could be nervous.

If your pony kicks, it's telling you it's annoyed or scared.

When your pony's ears are pricked up, it could just be listening to something but it could be sensing danger. If its ears are pinned flat back against its head, it might be angry.

When your pony lowers its head, it might want you, or another pony or horse to give it some space. Or it might just want a nap.

When ponies and horses sense danger, they run away.

Clicking its teeth is a way your pony will communicate with other horses and ponies.

GREAT GROOMING

Grooming your horse or pony is a great way to bond with them and also to keep them happy and healthy.

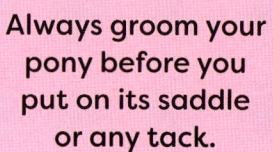

Always groom your pony before you put on its saddle or any tack.

Tie your pony up with a loose rope while grooming, so it can move around a bit if it wants to.

Your pony should enjoy being groomed, so try to be gentle and relaxed and your pony will be too.

If you pony is not happy about you grooming a certain area, it may be because it has a sore or cut there—so check carefully.

DID YOU KNOW?

Horses belong to the equine (*eh-kwine*) family that also includes zebras, donkeys, and giraffes.

GROOMING KIT

- ☐ body brush
- ☐ hoofpick
- ☐ curry comb
- ☐ dandy brush
- ☐ mane comb
- ☐ sweat scraper
- ☐ sponges

Check out this kit list for all you will need to groom your pony, then read on for some brushing know-how:

1 Use your rubber curry comb in small, circular motions. Start behind your pony's ears and finish at its tail. Don't use it on your pony's face or below the knees. The comb lifts dirt and dead skin cells to the top of your pony's coat.

2 Next use the stiffer dandy brush to remove the dirt with short flicks.

3 Smooth down your pony's coat with long, sweeping strokes, using your body brush.

4 Standing safely to one side, hold your pony's tail in one hand and use the other hand to get rid of any twigs before brushing the tail softly with your body brush.

Use your hoof pick to pick out any stones and dirt from your pony's hooves.

You should groom your pony every day, but if this is not possible, then three times a week.

After you've ridden your pony, grooming it helps it to dry off if it's sweaty, and stops it from getting cold and stiff.

HOME SWEET HOME

Check out these top tips to ensure your pony is happy in its home.

While a stable is important as a shelter, especially in the cold and rain, your pony needs to be able to roam free in a paddock or field for as long as possible each day.

Ponies make the best neighbors!

Ponies need to snack all the time, and should always have lots of grass or hay close by to graze on.

Your pony is a herd animal and will need to socialize with other ponies and horses in lots of space.

There are different styles of stables for ponies and horses. Traditional stables have lots of stables next to each other with doors that open out directly onto an open area.

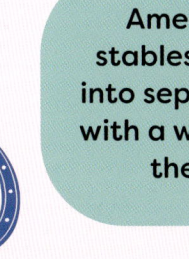

American Barn stables are divided into separate stables with a walkway down the middle.

Fencing is very important and should be checked often to make sure your pony is safe and secure.

21

PONY PEOPLE

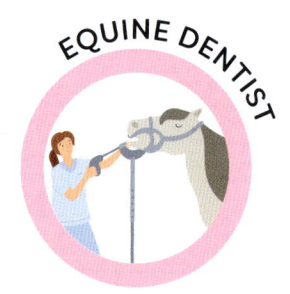

Keeping your pony happy and safe is not a one-person job, you'll need others to help you.

EQUINE DENTIST

SADDLE FITTER
As it grows, your pony's body will change shape and size so you will need to get its saddle checked and refitted if needed, once a year.

VET
Your pony's vet will take care of your pony when it is sick and give it any vaccinations it needs.

EQUINE DENTIST
Once or twice a year your pony will need to see a dentist to keep its teeth strong and healthy.

FARRIER
Your pony's hooves are very important and a farrier will help you take care of them.

INSTRUCTOR
You and your pony are never too old to have lessons with an expert and regular lessons will help you both improve.

YUM YUM!

Ponies and horses need to snack all day long, so they need plenty of healthy food to eat and water to drink.

Galloping around is thirsty work so your pony will need to drink lots of fresh, clean water throughout the day. Especially when it's hot.

Ponies graze around 18 hours a day. That's a lot of nibbling...so you need to make sure they have access to hay and grass all the time.

If your pony looks a bit thin, then add some extra horse feed to its daily diet. This contains things like sugar beet, oats, and nuts, which are good for it in small portions.

SLURRRP!

Carrots and apples make good healthy snacks for your pony, or try the easy recipe below for a tasty treat:

I carrot deny it...I love snacks!

1 Grate 2 carrots into a bowl and mix in 4 oz of porridge oats, 4 oz of flour, and 1 tablespoon of honey.

2 Mix together well then take a spoonful of mixture and mold it into a flattened ball and place onto a greased baking tray. Repeat with the rest of the mixture.

3 Bake in the oven at 375ºF for about 10 minutes, then leave to cool before feeding to your pony. Only one treat per day!

Ask a grown-up to help with tricky parts!

TOP TACK

Learn all about the equipment you will need to train and ride your pony.

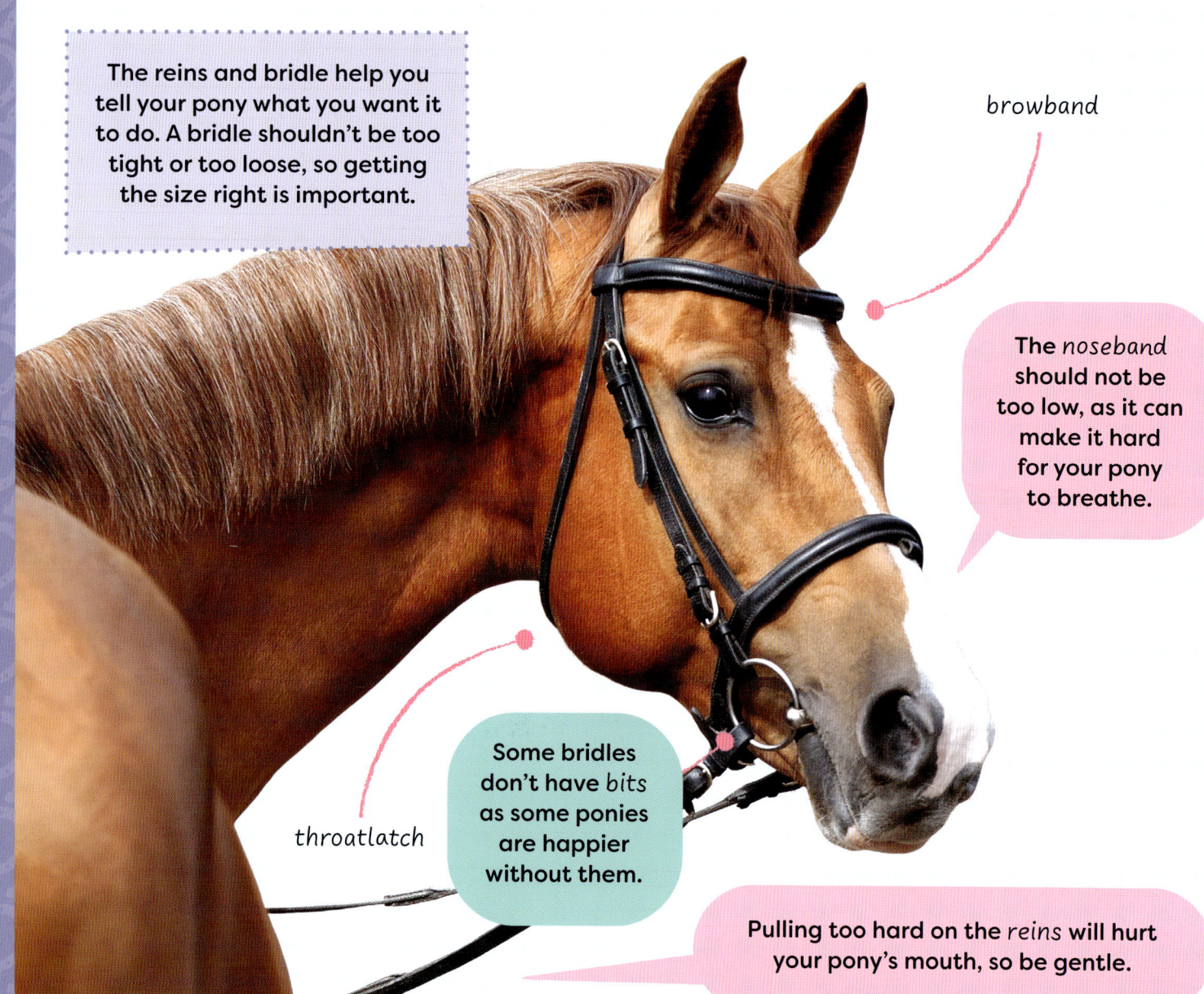

The reins and bridle help you tell your pony what you want it to do. A bridle shouldn't be too tight or too loose, so getting the size right is important.

browband

The *noseband* should not be too low, as it can make it hard for your pony to breathe.

throatlatch

Some bridles don't have *bits* as some ponies are happier without them.

Pulling too hard on the *reins* will hurt your pony's mouth, so be gentle.

You need to check your saddle every time before you ride your pony. You should also check the area of your pony's back that it sits on, in case there are any sores or cuts.

seat

pommel

skirt

Your saddle should be comfortable for you and your pony and, once in place, should not slip sideways.

knee roll

saddle flap

stirrup leather

stirrup iron

There are different kinds of saddles for dressage, jumping, and general riding.

DID YOU KNOW?

The Western saddle is bigger and heavier than the English saddle.

TRAINING TIPS

Read on to discover some top tips for training your pony.

Training a pony takes time. Be patient and don't expect to jump on and gallop off right away.

Be calm, confident, and happy when carrying out all your training. Your pony will pick up on any negative vibes.

Most ponies and horses shouldn't be ridden until they're between 2 and 4 years of age. Your vet will tell you if your pony or horse is ready to be ridden.

It's important you get your pony used to new places by leading it by the hand for a few weeks, before you start riding it.

Help your pony get used to its tack before you try riding with it on. Show your pony the noises the tack makes and how it feels against its body.

ha ha!
What's a pony's favorite game?

Stable tennis!

Reward your pony's good behavior right away with a treat. If there's a gap between its good behavior and your treat, your pony will not know when it has done what you wanted.

27

READY TO RIDE

How to prepare to ride your pony.

It's important to make your pony feel happy and relaxed before you start. Try giving your pony an apple or carrot to munch on. It will calm them down, and get them ready to ride.

Never forget these important points:

- Stay calm and relaxed, and it will help your pony stay calm too.
- Always wear a helmet!
- When you're calm, so am I!
- Proper riding boots will help, but you don't need them right away.
- Stay alert, and watch what your pony is doing, so you can stay in control.

MOUNTING YOUR PONY

1 Stand on the left side of the pony.

2 Step onto the mounting block, if you need one.

3 Hold the reins in your left hand.

4 Put your left foot in the stirrup, and stand up.

5 Swing your right leg over the pony's rump.

6 Sit down and put your right foot in the stirrup.

You're on!

GROUNDWORK

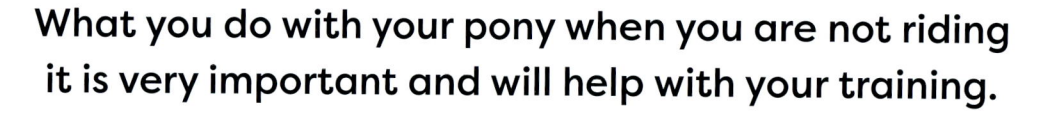

What you do with your pony when you are not riding it is very important and will help with your training.

You can teach your pony to speed up or slow down, by walking with it on a rope. The rope should be loose so neither you nor your pony are pulling on it.

Stroking and touching your pony on his head and body can be a reward for doing something right.

You can test how well you communicate with your pony by trying to get it to run or walk without any equipment. This is known as "working at liberty."

When leading your pony, stand on its left-hand side (also known as its near-side), next to its shoulder.

DID YOU KNOW?

Horses and ponies can sleep standing up. They lock their legs to keep from falling over.

SCRUB UP

A clean horse and tack means a happy horse and rider.

It is important to wash your tack after every ride to keep it soft, so it doesn't hurt your pony.

You can wash your tack with soap and water or saddle oil with water. Once washed, store it somewhere dry to keep it safe.

How many words can you make from the letters in the word HORSE?

sore
she

Tack that isn't cleaned regularly can crack, become stiff, and wear out—so keeping it clean will also help it last longer.

Answers could be: shore, he, sore, she, so, ore, hero, shoe, rose....

GIDDY UP!

When you learn to ride your pony, you will also learn to go at different speeds.

When your pony WALKS it does so with a four-beat gait (pattern). So all four of your pony's feet will lift up and land separately.

In a balanced walk, your pony's hind (back) hooves should fall into the hoofprints made by its front hooves.

DID YOU KNOW?

Outside legs are the horse's legs that are closest to the fence, when you're riding in an enclosed area. Inside legs are the ones closer to the center of the area.

A TROT is a bit quicker and is a two-beat gait. Every stride your pony takes will mean one of your pony's front feet will rise, along with the opposite back foot.

A CANTER is a three-beat gait. One back foot lands and pushes your pony upward, then the other back foot and opposite front foot land together, before the other front foot lands. When cantering sit up, with your shoulders back to keep your body upright.

True or false?

Horses don't have a belly button.

Answer: False. Like most mammals, horses do have a belly button.

THE GREAT OUTDOORS

Check out these top tips to make sure you always have a great ride with your pony.

When riding, always wear a hard hat to protect your head and make sure your coat is done up, so it doesn't flap and catch on your tack or distract your pony.

Riding with others is great fun for you and your pony. If your pony gets excited around other ponies though, start with a small group.

Ponies are herd animals and like to follow. Build up your pony's confidence to lead by walking alongside other ponies at first.

True or false?

A horse has amazing hearing and uses 10 muscles to control its ears.

Answer: TRUE

If you are riding in a busy area, always wear something hi-vis, which is something that can be seen by others.

ha ha!
What made the pony sad?

His pony pal's tail of *whoa!*

Never get angry or tell your pony off if it gets spooked, as this will only make it more nervous.

Be alert at all times and keep your eyes and ears open. Make sure your pony is concentrating too.

SHOWTIME

Once you've mastered walking, trotting, and cantering you can try out more challenging events with your pony.

The sport of eventing is a bit like a triathlon for horses, with three activities: dressage, cross country, and show jumping.

Show jumping is an event where horses and riders compete to clear a jumping course, with the lowest amount of faults in the fastest time.

When jumping, the rider needs to be able to control their horse and help it get to the exact spot where it needs to lift off from, to make the jump.

Cross country challenges a rider and horse to tackle lots of obstacles over different types of ground and water.

My jumping is truly neigh-mazing!

The horse needs to know how to hold a proper position over a jump, so it doesn't knock down the jump rails.

Dressage shows the great partnership between a horse and rider through a series of movements on the flat.

DID YOU KNOW?

Dressage is a French term that means training.

SUPER SPEED

Horse racing has been enjoyed since ancient times and is a popular sport all over the world.

Before a race, the jockeys (riders) must be weighed. If they are too light, lead weights must be added to their saddles so the race is fair.

The Kentucky Derby is one of the world's most famous horse races. It was first run in 1875 in Louisville, Kentucky. 20 horses compete in the race and the winning prize money is nearly 2 million dollars.

There are lots of different types of racing:
- Flat races take place on a level racecourse
- Steeplechase races are around a course with fences and ditches
- Harness racing is where horses pull a cart with a driver
- Maiden races are for horses that haven't won a race before

If you want to name a race horse, you have to send up to six names to the Jockey Club (a horse racing organization) to choose from. But you can't just pick any name. It must be shorter than 18 characters and unique.

DID YOU KNOW?

Younger riders can take part in pony races all over the world. A lot of jockeys start their riding careers racing ponies.

10 TIDY TIPS

Follow these top tips to keep your pony's home clean and tidy.

1 It's probably the worst part of pony care, but mucking out its poop is very important and should be done every day. Hold your breath if it helps!

2 Pick up poop from the fields your pony roams in.

3 Give the yard a good sweep, at least every couple of days to brush away all the dirt and grit that could get stuck in your pony's hooves.

4 Put all your tools and tack away neatly, to stop your yard from looking messy.

5 Make sure you clean out leaves or bits of food from your pony's water trough regularly.

6 Picking dirt out of your pony's hooves will keep its hooves and your yard clean.

7 Give your pony's food bucket a good scrub every day.

8 Keep your pony's water trough clean and healthy by giving it a good wash at least once a week.

9 Cobwebs gather dust which will affect your pony's breathing, so make sure you get rid of them when you spot a spider.

10 Once a month check your stable and yard's fences, stable doors, and gates to make sure everything is secure and not damaged.

SUPER STARS

Impress your friends with these fun facts about some of the world's most famous riders and horses.

Winning Brew became the fastest horse in 2008 at the Penn National Race Course, USA, setting a record at 43.97 mph.

The British rider **Charlotte Dujardin** and her horse **Valegro** hold the highest dressage score, an impressive 94.3%, achieved in London, England in 2014.

William Steinkraus was born in 1925 and was the first US rider to win an Olympic horse-event gold medal. He rode on the US team for 22 years.

Alberto Larraguibel Morales and his horse Huaso performed the highest jump—8 feet, 1¼ inches—in 1949 in Santiago, Chile.

JJS Summer Breeze, from Kansas, USA, broke the world record for the longest tail in 2007. Her flowing locks measured 150 inches.

HEALTHY HORSES

Check out these top tips to keep your pony healthy.

Where does a horse go when it feels unwell?

Horsepital! Ha ha!

★ A healthy horse and pony should be alert with its ears pricked back or up.

★ Your pony's coat should be shiny and smooth, not greasy to touch.

★ Just like humans, weepy eyes or a runny nose are a sign your pony isn't feeling well, so if you spot these, call the vet.

★ If your pony is not eating much, it could mean it is unwell.

★ If your pony keeps bolting or rearing up when you ride, it could be a sign of dental problems.

Make sure you keep your pony up to date with its vaccines, which will protect it from harmful diseases.

HOW TO DRAW A PONY

Follow these simple steps to learn how to draw a pony, then practise in the space below.

1. Draw these three simple shapes first.

2. Add lines for the head, neck, tail, mane, and foreleg.

3. Sketch out the other legs and saddle like this.

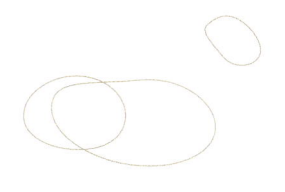

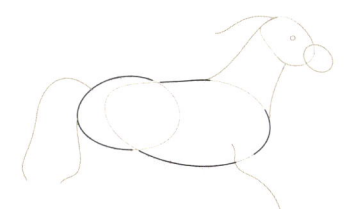

4. Add details of the head, saddle, tail, and mane.

5. Complete the outline of the pony like this.

6. Colour in with pencils or pens.

MY PERFECT PONY

Fill in this page with all the things that make your pony great. If you don't have your own pony, use the space to plan your dream one.

Name:

Breed:

Mane color:

Tail color:

Circle 3 words to describe your pony (or how you would like your pony to be):

calm	lively	mischievous
slow	noisy	obedient
gentle	friendly	fast

When I neigh, I end up a little hoarse.

Circle everything your pony likes (or your dream pony might like):

hugs	jumping	walking
cantering	galloping	other ponies
trotting	snacks	napping

Tick 3 things your pony likes to eat (or would like to eat).

oats	hay
apple	grass
carrot	grain

ha ha!
What sort of horses come out after dark?

Nightmares!

Draw you and your (dream) pony here.

Number these animals from 1 to 6, with 1 for the one you like most to 6, for the one you like least.

pony	☐	hamster	☐
cat	☐	fish	☐
dog	☐	rabbit	☐

The publishers would like to thank the following sources for their kind permission to reproduce the pictures in this book.

2, 4–6, 8, 10–13, 14, 16, 18–21, 24–32, 34, 36-37, 40, 44, 46 Mary Luts/Shutterstock; 4, 5, 43 Darq/Shutterstock; 4, 6, 8, 11, 14, 47 Rita_Kochmarjova/Shutterstock; 5, 14 SeventyFour/Shutterstock; 5, 48 Kwadrat/Shutterstock; 5, 18 wavebreakmedia/Shutterstock; 5, 22 Christin Noelle/Shutterstock; 6 OlesyaNickolaevautterstock; 7 Ahturner/Shutterstock; 8 skmj/Shutterstock; 8 Jonathan Densford/Alamy; 9 Jaco Wiid/Shutterstock; 9 Juniors Bildarchiv GmbH/Alamy; 10 Callipso88/Shutterstock; 10 Nancy Kennedy/Shutterstock; 10 PaySides/Shutterstock; 10 Olga_i/Shutterstock; 10 Mark J. Barrett/Alamy Stock Photo; 10 Sheree Sedgbeer/Alamy Stock Photo; 11, 16–17 Juniors Bildarchiv GmbH/Alamy Stock Photo; 11 Alessandra Sarti/Alamy Stock Photo; 11 bob langrish/Alamy Stock Photo; 11 Kemphoto countryside/animals/Alamy Stock Photo; 11 Abramova Kseniya/Shutterstock; 12-13 Callipso88/Shutterstock; 12 Eric Isselee/Shutterstock; 12-13 Midstream/Shutterstock; 13 Skalapendra/Shutterstock; 15 Zoltan Totka/Shutterstock; 16 Kwadrat/Shutterstock; 17 Wendy Perry/Shutterstock; 19 Eric Gevaert/Shutterstock; 19 Marek Rybar/Shutterstock; 20 Groomee/Shutterstock; 21 ILiyan/Shutterstock; 21 Nikoner/Shutterstock; 21 Tibesty/Shutterstock; 22 hedgehog94/Shutterstock; 22 MarienAvery/Shutterstock; 23 Lilac Mountain/Shutterstock; 23 Iocrifa/Shutterstock; 24 Edoma/Shutterstock; 25 Alexey Wraith/Shutterstock; 26 freya-photographer/Shutterstock; 26 Pressmaster/Shutterstock; 27 Elena Elisseeva/Alamy Stock Photo; 27 AnnaElizabeth Photography/Alamy Stock Photo; 28 PeopleImages.com - Yuri A/Shutterstock; 29 cynoclub/Shutterstock; 30 Gelpi/Shutterstock; 31 AnnaElizabeth photography/Shutterstock; 32 Rolf Dannenberg/Shutterstock; 33 Mandy Peake/Shutterstock; 34 Sally Anderson/Alamy Stock Photo; 34 Alzay/Shutterstock; 35 Dennis whiting/Shutterstock; 35 mazur serhiy UA/Shutterstock; 36 Sergii Kumer/Shutterstock; 37 christopher jones/Alamy Stock Photo; 37 Simon Bratt/Shutterstock; 38–39 Jim Noetzel/Shutterstock; 40 Elena Elisseeva/Shutterstock; 41 AnnaElizabeth photography/Shutterstock; 41 Richard Juilliart/Shutterstock; 42 Sipa US/Alamy Stock Photo; 43 GRANGER - Historical Picture Archive/Alamy Stock Photo; 44 otsphoto/Shutterstock; 44 hedgehog94/Shutterstock; 45 Cernecka Natalja/Shutterstock; 46 Petr Jelinek/Shutterstock.

Every effort has been made to acknowledge correctly and contact the source and/or copyright holder of each picture and Welbeck Publishing Group apologises for any unintentional errors or omissions, which will be corrected in future editions of this book.